patterns for fun

Book 1

Paul Sheftel and Vera Wills

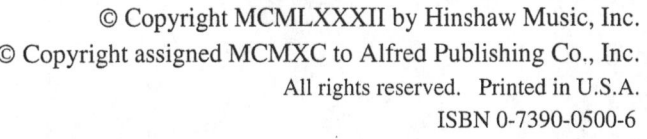

© Copyright MCMLXXXII by Hinshaw Music, Inc.
© Copyright assigned MCMXC to Alfred Publishing Co., Inc.
All rights reserved.   Printed in U.S.A.

ISBN 0-7390-0500-6

Contents

climbing

Building Blocks

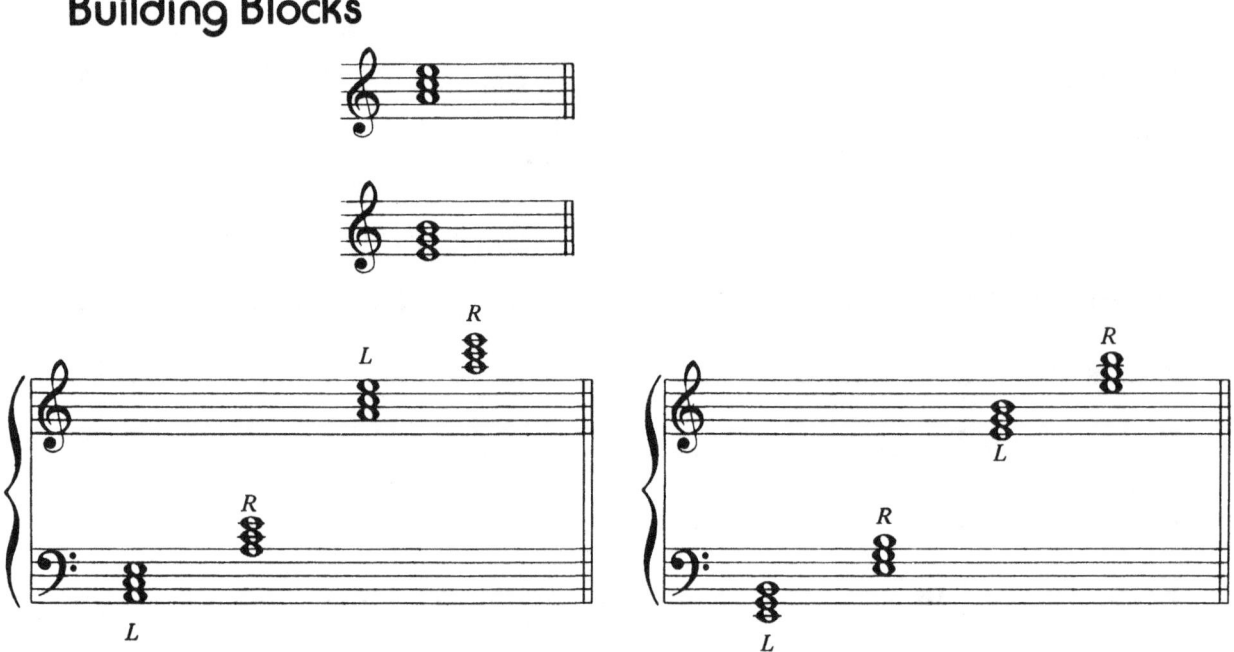

- This piece consists of two elements: (1) the building blocks played as arpeggios, and (2) two finger patterns: 1-5, 1-5; 1-2-3-4-5.

- Measures 11 and 12: play the A minor arpeggio six times, crossing hands, plus the ending note.

Activity

- Use the left pedal *(una corda)* throughout and play as softly as possible.

climbing

swooping blues

Building Blocks

- Chords — 1. C minor — C major
  - 2. F minor — F major
  - 3. G minor — G major

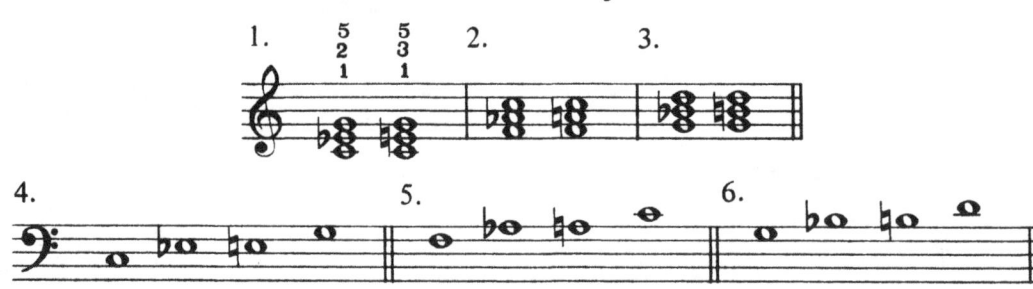

Comments

- The left hand plays only bottom and top notes of chords in broken form (measure 1), or as open 5ths (measure 3).

- Measure 3. Notice how this pattern grows out of building block 4.

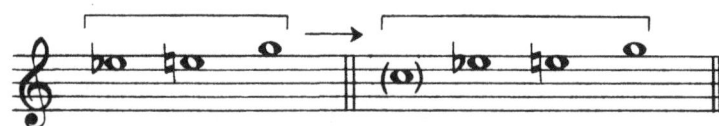

Activity

- Go up the C major scale, transposing measure 1 on each key:

etc.

swooping blues

oops!

Building Blocks

● C major scale in contrary motion.

Patterns

● Finger pattern—1-2-3   1-2-3-4-5. Learn right hand, then hands together.
● Finger pattern—5-2-3-2

● Finger pattern—5-1-2-1

● Right and left hands use same fingering throughout piece.

Comments

● Be careful of skip from 5th to 3rd finger in measure 11.

Activity

● Play *Oops* starting with the thumbs on any white key. Use only white keys.

● Play in G major. To do this you must use F♯ .

oops!

subdominant blues

Building Blocks

Form

- *Subdominant Blues* follows a basic 12-bar blues pattern. It is best to think in four-measure groupings.

  C — 4 measures

  F — 2 measures
  C — 2 measures

  G — 1 measure
  F — 1 measure
  C — 2 measures

  C — 1 measure (ending)

Preparation

- Tap out the following rhythm:

Here is the same rhythm divided between the hands:

Comments

- Fingering for chords —

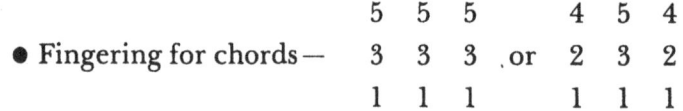

5	5	5		4	5	4
3	3	3	or	2	3	2
1	1	1		1	1	1

subdominant blues

Play l.h. 1 octave lower throughout

fifths and starts

Building Blocks

Comments

- The left-hand drone should be felt in groups of four.

- Practice the right-hand building blocks, first as written, and then with the added fifths.

- *pppp* means as softly as humanly possible, or possibly softer.

Activity

- Mix up the right-hand building blocks to create an improvisation. Keep the left-hand drone going.

- To build the longest, loudest *crescendo* possible, keep repeating measure 13 as long as you wish.

fifths and starts

reflections

Building Blocks

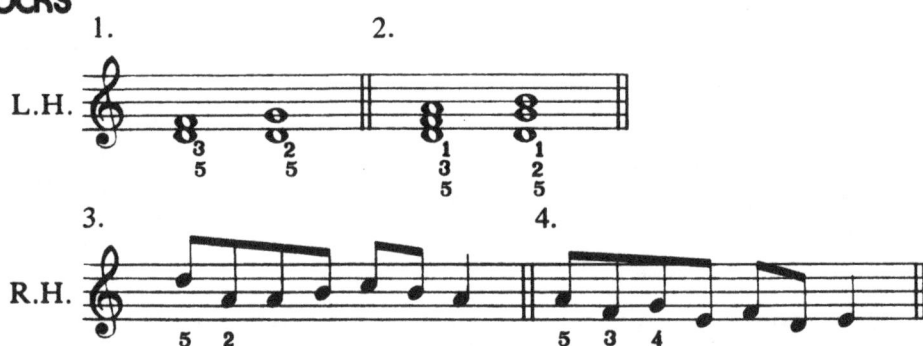

Activity

- Play building blocks 3 and 4 in any order. Accompany using either or both of the left-hand building blocks. Create an improvisation by playing in different registers on the keyboard.

- The mirror image of the building block can be obtained by playing the right-hand melody with the left hand in contrary motion as illustrated.

From this, two new building blocks are obtained which can be added to the improvisation.

reflections

four-finger blues

Building Blocks

Form

- *Four-Finger Blues* follows a basic 12-bar blues pattern. It is best to think in four-measure groupings.

  C — 4 measures

  F — 2 measures
  C — 2 measures

  G — 1 measure
  F — 1 measure
  C — 2 measures

four-finger blues

contrasts

Building Blocks

- D minor chord   F♯ major chord (right and left hands)

Patterns

- Block chords   —hands crossing over.

- Block chords   —hands together.

- Broken chords—interlocking pattern, descending (measures 5 and 6).

- Block chords   —alternating chords with staccato touch (measures 7 and 8).

Comments

- Have left foot ready on "left" pedal *(una corda)* before starting.

- Where ℘ed. and *una corda* are indicated use right and left pedals simultaneously.

contrasts

*una corda = left pedal

sixth-sense blues

Building Blocks

1. 2. 3. 4.

Comments

- The following exercise is suggested for building blocks 1 and 4.

R.H.

- Tap out the rhythm of measure 2 before playing.

First *without* tied note: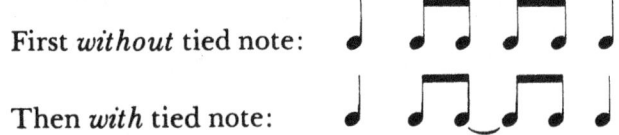

Then *with* tied note: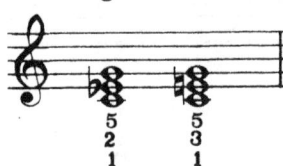

- Building block 3 can be understood as a C minor — C major chord:

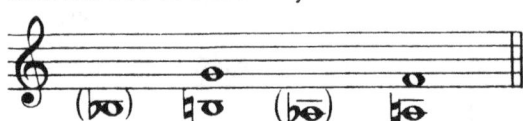

- Measure 14. The student can locate the white-key 6ths first, then add the lower black keys:

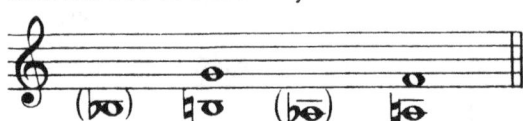

sixth-sense blues

dominant-seventh heaven

Building Blocks

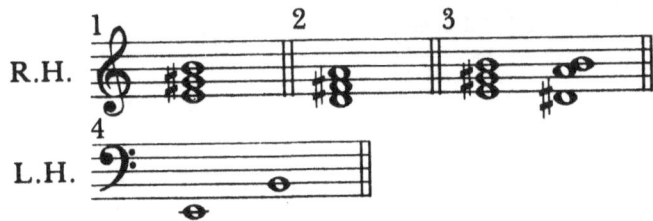

Preparation

- Measure 1. First tap out the rhythm with one hand, then divide between left and right as indicated:

- Measure 4. The E major chord is outlined with the addition of G natural.

- Measure 9. This can be understood as an extension of measure 4.

dominant-seventh heaven

second-position blues

Building Blocks

Form

- *Second-Position Blues* follows a basic twelve-bar blues pattern. It is best to think in four-measure groupings:

  C — 4 measures

  F — 2 measures
  C — 2 measures

  G — 1 measure
  F — 1 measure
  C — 2 measures

Activity

- Play a C major chord in the first position and practice going to the second as fast as possible.

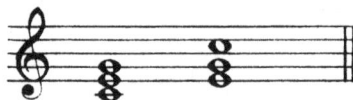

- Now try this with an F major, then a G major chord.

- Try the same activity starting on D major, A major, and E major chords. (First position has one black key in the middle.)

second-position blues

progression rock

Preparation

- Measures 1–4. There are three basic chords:

- Each basic chord has a variant (only one note changes):

- Measures 5–6. Basic chords:

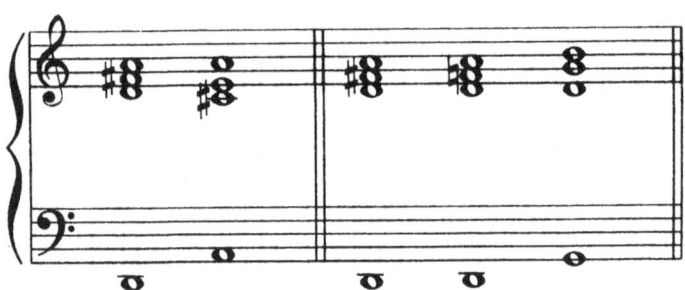

- Measures 5–6. Tap out the rhythmic pattern:

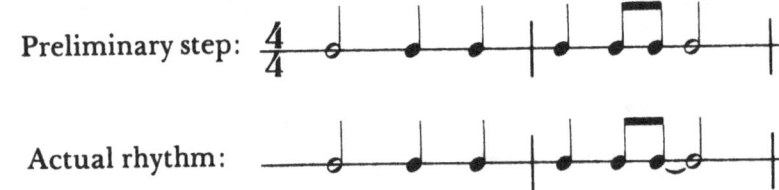

progression rock

chromatics

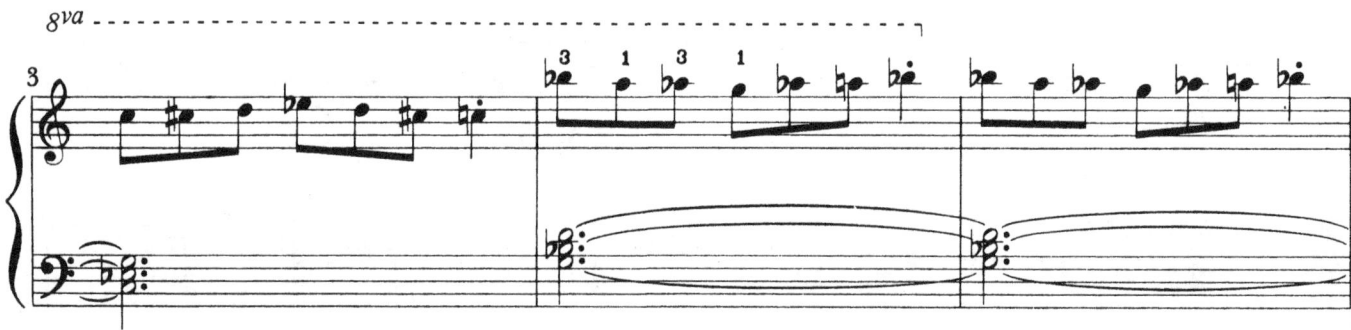

Chromatic scale all the way to the end of keyboard!

chromatics

Preparation

- Right-hand chromatic scale.

- Use only 1-2-3 fingers. Third finger is always and only on the black keys.

Building Blocks

- In the right hand there is only one building block, with two variants:

1. (basic)   2. (variant)

3. (variant)

About the Authors

Paul Sheftel, author of *Blues for Fun, Patterns for Fun, Plays the Thing* and other works for piano, began his musical studies at the age of four in Los Angeles, California, where one of his teachers was the noted composer Mario Castelnuovo-Tedesco. Later he studied in Paris under Lazare Levy and Alexandre Tansman. He earned his B.S. and M.S. degrees at the Juilliard School in New York, where he studied with Edward Stenerman, then received a Fulbright grant for two years of study at the Santa Cecilia Conservatory in Rome. As part of the two-piano team, Rollino and Sheftel, he has appeared as soloist with the Concertgebouw Orchestra of Amsterdam, the Hague and Rotterdam Philharmonics, the Berlin Philharmonic, the Royal Philharmonic of London and the Chicago Symphony. Rollino and Sheftel were soloists in the world premiere of Hans Werner Henze's *Muses of Sicily*. They also performed in the world premier of Gunther Schuller's Concerto for Two Pianos and Orchestra.

Paul is well known as a lecturer and gives frequent workshops throughout the country.

Vera Wills is a lively and imaginative composer and teacher of piano pedagogy. Her creative insights to piano teaching have given new direction to the lives and careers of countless teachers who have attended her seminars at the Mannes College of Music in New York City, where for many years she has lectured as a member of the piano faculty. She studied with distinguished teachers at Hunter College of Music and the Peabody Conservatory.

Vera has held many elected posts, including that of president of the Piano Teachers Congress of New York, Inc., and chairperson for District 1 of the New York State Music Teachers Association. She has composed and arranged music for the Merry Wanderers' Children's Theatre in New York. She maintains a busy schedule composing imaginative piano books for children, as well as pedagogy books for teachers.